ALL AROUND THE WORLD
SOMALIA

by Kristine Spanier, MLIS

pogo

Ideas for Parents and Teachers

Pogo Books let children practice reading informational text while introducing them to nonfiction features such as headings, labels, sidebars, maps, and diagrams, as well as a table of contents, glossary, and index.

Carefully leveled text with a strong photo match offers early fluent readers the support they need to succeed.

Before Reading

- "Walk" through the book and point out the various nonfiction features. Ask the student what purpose each feature serves.
- Look at the glossary together. Read and discuss the words.

Read the Book

- Have the child read the book independently.
- Invite him or her to list questions that arise from reading.

After Reading

- Discuss the child's questions. Talk about how he or she might find answers to those questions.
- Prompt the child to think more. Ask: Many people in Somalia move from place to place. Would you prefer to move your home, or do you like staying in one place?

Pogo Books are published by Jump!
5357 Penn Avenue South
Minneapolis, MN 55419
www.jumplibrary.com

Library of Congress Cataloging-in-Publication Data

Names: Spanier, Kristine, author.
Title: Somalia / Kristine Spanier.
Description: Minneapolis, MN: Jump!, Inc., 2021.
Series: All around the world | Includes index.
Audience: Ages 7-10 | Audience: Grades 2-3
Identifiers: LCCN 2019047613 (print)
LCCN 2019047614 (ebook)
ISBN 9781645273561 (hardcover)
ISBN 9781645273578 (paperback)
ISBN 9781645273585 (ebook)
Subjects: LCSH: Somalia—Juvenile literature.
Classification: LCC DT401.5 .S73 2021 (print)
LCC DT401.5 (ebook) | DDC 967.73—dc23
LC record available at https://lccn.loc.gov/2019047613
LC ebook record available at https://lccn.loc.gov/2019047614

Editor: Jenna Gleisner
Designer: Molly Ballanger

Photo Credits: Kalik Ahmed/Shutterstock, cover; Eric Lafforgue/Art in All of Us/Getty, 1; Pixfiction/Shutterstock, 3; Michael Runkel/robertharding/SuperStock, 4; Victor Modesto/Shutterstock, 5; Mike Goldwater/Alamy, 6-7; Mark Pearson/Alamy, 8-9; esfera/Shutterstock, 10l; ZUMA Press, Inc./Alamy, 10r; Karel Prinsloo/AP Images, 11; MDOGAN/Shutterstock, 12-13; donikz/Shutterstock, 14; Free Wind 2014/Shutterstock, 15; Xinhua/Alamy, 16-17; Africa Collection/Alamy, 18-19; Peter Turnley/Getty, 20-21; Anton_Ivanov/Shutterstock, 23.

Printed in the United States of America at Corporate Graphics in North Mankato, Minnesota.

TABLE OF CONTENTS

CHAPTER 1

WELCOME TO SOMALIA!

What country is in the horn of Africa? Somalia! This country has 2,071 miles (3,333 kilometers) of **coastline**! Welcome!

Paintings are on the walls of the Laas Geel caves. They are more than 5,000 years old! They show cattle and other animals.

Many people in Somalia live as **nomads**. They travel from place to place. Why? They care for cattle, camels, and other **livestock**. They move to find water and better **pastures** for their animals.

The Jubba River is here. So is the Shabelle River. They are good sources of water. Farmers grow bananas, sugarcane, and rice. Grapefruit, mangoes, and papayas are other **crops** grown here.

DID YOU KNOW?

The **climate** is hot and dry. Sometimes there are **droughts**. This makes it hard to grow enough food for people to eat.

crops

CHAPTER 2

A COUNTRY'S STRUGGLES

Mohamed Siad Barre took power in 1969. He was a **dictator**. A **civil war** broke out. Barre was **overthrown** in 1991. The people of Somalia suffered because of the war.

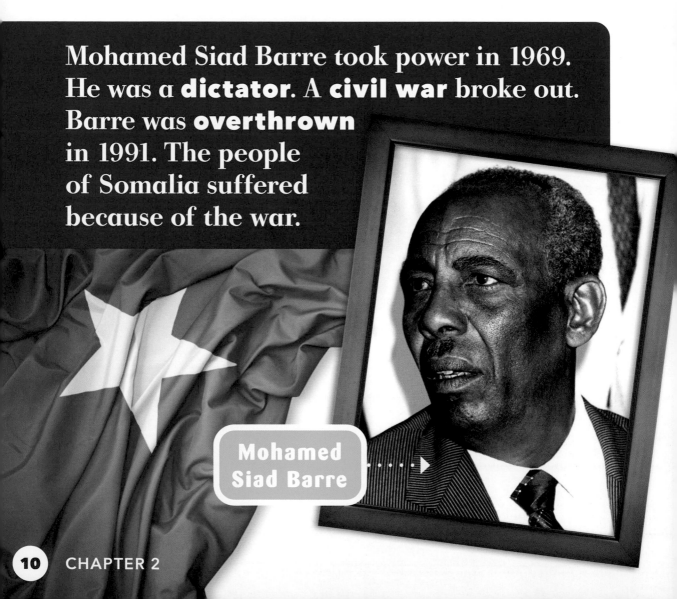

Mohamed Siad Barre

A **tsunami** in the Indian Ocean hit the coast in 2004. More than 275 people died. Many more lost their homes. People here continue to struggle because of **famine**.

The government is working to make the country safer. It meets in Mogadishu. This is the **capital**. It is also the largest city here.

Mogadishu

TAKE A LOOK!

The flag of Somalia looks simple. But it has important meaning. What does the star mean to the people?

■ = sky and Indian Ocean

☆ star of **unity** = five **regions** in Africa where Somali people have lived

CHAPTER 3

PEOPLE IN SOMALIA

Would you like to try a sambusa? This is a fried pastry. It is filled with spicy meat or vegetables. Rice cooked in a meat broth is a tasty meal. Flatbread is served at every meal.

sambusa ·····▶

People travel on buses, trucks, or minibuses in cities. In **rural** areas, people ride on camels, cattle, or donkeys. Animals help carry belongings.

It is hard to go to school in Somalia. There are not enough buildings or teachers in rural areas. School supplies are expensive. Children who live in cities may go to religious schools. Some attend private schools.

WHAT DO YOU THINK?

Some children are needed at home to help with work. This keeps them from going to school. Are you able to go to school every day? How would you feel if you couldn't go?

Most people here are Muslim. Ramadan is an important holiday. Eid al-Fitr is celebrated at the end. This is a time to feast. People exchange gifts. Eid al-Adha is also celebrated. It is a time to share with others.

Telling stories is **a tradition** here. Why? The Somali language did not have a written alphabet until 1972. People love to tell family stories and myths. They also enjoy singing and dancing together.

There is a lot to know about this country. Would you like to learn more?

WHAT DO YOU THINK?

Passing on stories is an example of a family tradition. What traditions does your family have? Are they similar to what your friends do? Are they different?

QUICK FACTS & TOOLS

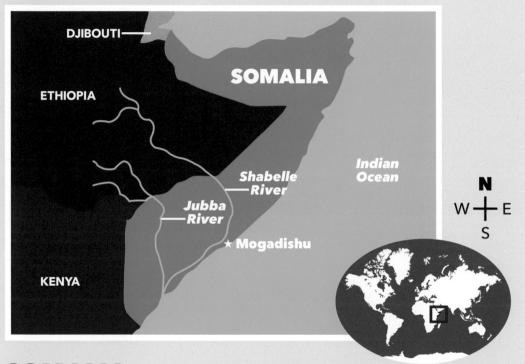

SOMALIA

Location: East Africa

Size: 246,200 square miles (637,655 square kilometers)

Population: 11,259,029 (July 2018 estimate)

Capital: Mogadishu

Type of Government: federal parliamentary republic

Languages: Somali, Arabic, Italian, English

Exports: livestock, bananas, fish, charcoal

Currency: Somali shilling

GLOSSARY

capital: A city where government leaders meet.

civil war: A war between different groups within the same country.

climate: The weather typical of a certain place over a long period of time.

coastline: The area where land meets the ocean.

crops: Plants grown for food.

dictator: A ruler who has complete control of a country, often by force.

droughts: Long periods without rain.

famine: A serious lack of food in a geographic area.

livestock: Animals that are kept or raised on a farm or ranch.

nomads: People who wander from place to place.

overthrown: To have been forced from power.

pastures: Grazing lands for animals.

regions: General areas or specific districts or territories.

rural: Related to the country and country life.

tradition: A custom, idea, or belief that is handed down from one generation to the next.

tsunami: A very large, destructive wave caused by an underwater earthquake or volcano.

unity: The state of being united or joined as a whole.

Somalia's currency

INDEX

TO LEARN MORE

Finding more information is as easy as 1, 2, 3.

1 Go to www.factsurfer.com

2 Enter "Somalia" into the search box.

3 Click the "Surf" button to see a list of websites.

FACT SURFER